The New York Times

MINI CROSSWORDS VOLUME 2

The New York Times

MINI CROSSWORDS:
150 Easy Fun-Sized Puzzles
Volume 2

By Joel Fagliano

ST. MARTIN'S GRIFFIN ❧ NEW YORK

The New York Times

MINI CROSSWORDS VOLUME 2

Looking for more Easy Crosswords?

Introduction

When you think about it, crosswords are particularly well-suited for our fast-paced, modern age. Almost every clue and answer is on a different subject, your mind bounces from one thing to the next, and when a puzzle's not too hard, it takes only a short time to do.

Well, if regular crosswords are modern, *The New York Times*'s new Mini crosswords are hypermodern. The clues and answers are just as diverse, but each 5×5-square grid takes a mere minute or so to complete—even less once you get good. You now feel the rush of excitement in finishing a puzzle in a fraction of the time!

Launched in 2014, and originally available only digitally, the Mini has become so popular that now on weekdays it also appears in print in the main section of the paper.

Each Mini is created by Joel Fagliano, the paper's digital crosswords editor, who started selling regular crosswords to the *Times* when he was seventeen. To date he's had more than 50 weekday and Sunday crosswords published in the paper, becoming in the process one of the most popular and accomplished puzzlemakers.

Joel packs his Minis with lively vocabulary, modern references, and the sort of playfulness and intelligence you'll find in its big brother elsewhere in the paper. The Minis are easy/medium in difficulty. The cultural references skew young. But don't let the small size and big squares fool you. These puzzles are decidedly for adults.

On the following pages are 150 Minis from the *Times*, lightly re-edited for their first publication in book form.

Let the many rushes of excitement begin!

—Will Shortz

¹	²	³	■	⁴
⁵			⁶	
⁷				
⁸				
	■	⁹		

ACROSS

1 Smokey the Bear ad, e.g., for short

5 "Sup"

7 Robert De Niro in "Meet the Fockers," e.g.

8 Where a witness testifies, with "the"

9 "Sup"

DOWN

1 _____ Food (Ben & Jerry's flavor named after a band)

2 Already in the mail

3 God of the Koran

4 "Sup"

6 Highway division

1	2	3		4
5				
6			7	
		8		
9				

ACROSS

1 Overdone glamour
5 What Eve was formed from
6 Mercer beating Duke in the 2014 March Madness, e.g.
8 ____ rock (genre for Jimmy Eat World)
9 Tear-out from Playboy magazine

DOWN

1 Grouchy guy
2 Part of the mouth
3 "A Doll's House" playwright
4 Last band in the Rock and Roll Hall of Fame, alphabetically
7 Flightless bird

1	**2**	**3**	**4**	**5**
6				
7				
8				
9				■

ACROSS

1 With 1-Down, smoothie chain with a Mango-a-go-go flavor
6 Civil War side, with "the"
7 Snow-block home
8 Seafood offering
9 Forever and ever

DOWN

1 See 1-Across
2 The "A" of WASP
3 Italian city with a semiannual fashion week
4 Sounds from supersonic planes
5 Spanish years

4

	1	2	3	4
5				
6				
7				
8				

ACROSS

1 Late comic Rivers
5 Increase in troop levels
6 "Yeah . . . so that wasn't totally true"
7 Columbia athletes
8 Philosopher Immanuel who wrote "Critique of Pure Reason"

DOWN

1 Louis-Dreyfus of "Veep"
2 Constellation with a belt
3 Actor's representative
4 Nickelodeon's "___ Declassified School Survival Guide"
5 ___ Road (online black market shut down by the F.B.I.)

ACROSS

1 Saffron or sage
4 Chat program whose logo is a yellow stick figure
6 State of nervous excitement
8 Opposite of con
9 Prominent St. Louis landmark

DOWN

1 Start of a Web address
2 Stubble remover
3 Show ___ (Hollywood industry)
5 The Great Wall of China being visible from space, e.g.
7 401(k) alternative

6

ACROSS

1 Where 8-Across store pollen
4 Moo ___ pork
5 What 8-Across beat about 200 times a second
7 Small, low island
8 Theme of this puzzle

DOWN

1 Greek letter X
2 Postal scale unit
3 Like 8-Across, in a saying
4 Mop, as the deck
6 Hydrogen or helium

1	**2**	**3**		**4**
5			■	
6			**7**	
	■	**8**		
9				

ACROSS

1 Shaggy's nickname for his dog

5 First part of a famous elocution phrase

6 Have because of

8 Part 2 of the phrase

9 Boxer with a cameo in "The Hangover"

DOWN

1 Photo _____ (model's session)

2 Part 4 of the phrase

3 Jesse _____, hero of the Berlin Olympics

4 Part 3 of the phrase

7 "Not _____ shabby!"

8

	1	2	3	
4				5
6				
7				
	8			

ACROSS

1 Show of affection
4 Sum of any two opposite faces on a standard die
6 Demotion victim of 2006
7 Grade point average booster
8 Oozy tree output

DOWN

1 Lends a hand
2 Lump in one's throat?
3 "C'mon, sleepyhead!"
4 Place that might offer mud baths
5 What horizontal head shakes signify

	1	2	3	
4				5
6				
7				
	8			

ACROSS

1 Valedictorian's pride, for short
4 Search for natural gas, in a way
6 Crucial artery
7 Lone minority, in modern lingo
8 Bananas, nuts or crackers

DOWN

1 Bride's partner
2 Cold-weather jacket
3 Performed on Broadway, say
4 What the "gras" of "Mardi Gras" means
5 "The Wizard of Oz" locale: Abbr.

10

1	2	3	4	5
6				
7				
8				
9				

ACROSS

1 British _____ (Great Britain, Ireland, etc.)
6 Target competitor
7 The N in "TNT"
8 Animal that eats while floating on its back
9 Overrun with dandelions and such

DOWN

1 "You're preaching to the choir!"
2 Strike down, Biblically
3 Drink that may feature "foam art"
4 Committed a faux pas
5 Reporter's pursuit

1		2	3	
		4		5
6	7			
8				
	9			

ACROSS

1 Figure in the Twitter logo
4 Clumsy idiot
6 Ancient kingdom on the Nile
8 Figure in the Snapchat logo
9 Eye affliction

DOWN

1 Google rival
2 Figure in the Android logo
3 "She loves me, she loves me not" flower
5 Destiny
7 Sounds of uncertainty

ACROSS

1 "The New Yorker" piece
5 Author Veronica of the "Divergent" trilogy
6 Author John of "The Fault in Our Stars"
8 Animal milk source
9 ___ Lauren (clothing label)

DOWN

1 Unit of energy, in physics
2 Kinda
3 Danielle who's the best-selling author alive
4 Oodles
7 To the ___ degree

ACROSS

1 Where people may get into hot water?
4 Super Bowl XLIX team, to fans
7 "To whom ___ concern"
8 11th-grade exams, for short
9 "All the news that's fit to print" initials

DOWN

1 Use FedEx or UPS
2 Super Bowl XLIX team, to fans
3 "For cryin' out loud!"
5 Perry who performed at the Super Bowl XLIX halftime show
6 The "S" of GPS: Abbr.

14

1	2	3	4	5
6				
7				
8				
9				

ACROSS

1 Hindu garments
6 "Let's not fight anymore, ok?"
7 Golf legend Palmer, informally
8 Like much Seattle weather
9 Company behind FarmVille and Words With Friends

DOWN

1 HBO competitor
2 Impressive display
3 Brush with the law
4 What "Happy Anniversary!" may be written with
5 "I'm outta here!"

ACROSS

1 Robin's egg color
4 Debt acknowledgment
5 Substances taken by A-Rod
7 Part of LGBT
8 British pound, informally

DOWN

1 Scarer's shout
2 One of the Mario Brothers
3 "Careful, now!"
4 "The Hurt Locker" setting
6 Many a Little League coach

1	2	3	4	
5				6
7				
8				
	9			

ACROSS

1 Ewes' guys
5 First one-term U.S. president
7 See 3-Down
8 ___ Eight (March Madness round)
9 Many a fake ID user

DOWN

1 Topic of a landmark 2008 speech by candidate Obama
2 Full-price payer at the movies
3 With 7-Across, first woman to win a Nobel Prize
4 Strike, in the Bible
6 Witnessed

1	2	3	4	■
5				6
7				
8				
■	9			

ACROSS

1 Skinny
5 "The Grand Budapest ___" (2015 Best Picture nominee)
7 Blown away
8 2015 Best Picture nominee
9 Like Easter eggs

DOWN

1 "___ Is Why I'm Hot," 2007 #1 hit
2 Perfected
3 Country with a green, white and red flag
4 Self-description after turning over a new leaf
6 Be in front

18

1	**2**	**3**	**4**	
5				**6**
7				
8				
	9			

ACROSS

1 2007 title role for Ellen Page
5 Geologic time unit
7 Like much Szechuan cuisine
8 Word with truth or blood
9 Bruce ____, 2013 Best Actor nominee for "Nebraska"

DOWN

1 The new girl on Fox's "New Girl"
2 Increased
3 Bête ____ (pet peeve)
4 Come to pass
6 "Amazing Grace" or "To God Be the Glory"

1		**2**	**3**	**4**
	■	**5**		
6	**7**			
8			■	
9				

ACROSS

1 America's favorite food, per a 2014 USDA study

5 Turkey piece

6 O_3

8 Gotham City searchlight symbol

9 Land on the Suez Canal

DOWN

1 Government investigation

2 Ruble : Russia :: _____ : Poland

3 Branch of Buddhism

4 Word after chemical, double or secret

7 Veer back in the other direction

ACROSS

2 ___ in xylophone (spelling clarification)
5 Palindromic half of an African capital
7 Palindromic belief
8 Palindromic data
9 Mac platform

DOWN

1 Unkind nickname for a tubby guy
2 Palindromic antianxiety pill
3 Help with a crime
4 Focus of some H.S. prep courses
6 "All ___ are off!"

ACROSS

1 Split (up)
5 Dark purple fruit
6 Overly angry, in modern slang
8 Feast at which mahimahi might be served
9 Hamlet's word before "perchance to dream"

DOWN

1 Marx's "____ Kapital"
2 Poker declaration
3 Appraiser's figure
4 Curriculum ____
7 "I'm with ya"

1	2	3	4	5
6				
7				
8				
9				

ACROSS

1 Pat down, as for weapons
6 Designer Oscar de la ___
7 Follow, as advice
8 "That's never gonna happen"
9 Hundred-dollar bill, slangily

DOWN

1 Parisian money before the euro
2 Military info-gathering
3 Divided down the middle
4 Brown weasel-like animal
5 "Yeezus" rapper

	1	2	3	4
5				
6				
7				
8				

ACROSS

1 Bamboozle
5 Like tabloid headlines
6 Joint below the tibia
7 About 71% of the earth's surface
8 Narcissist's love

DOWN

1 ___ cap: idiot's wear
2 Nerdy neighbor on "Family Matters"
3 Spiced rice dish
4 Adam and Eve's garden
5 Myanmar neighbor

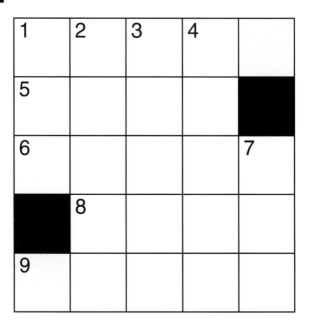

ACROSS

1 Chocolate bean
5 Hit or miss
6 Prepared to sing the national anthem
8 Paper or plastic
9 One getting the sack in December?

DOWN

1 Rite Aid competitor
2 Insurance giant
3 Sing like Frank Ocean or Michael Bublé
4 "All ____ That Bass," 2015 Grammy Song of the Year nominee
7 Double-helix material

ACROSS

1 Unexpected issue
5 Thin curl of smoke
6 Engineers' schools, for short
7 Alcoholic beverage made from rice
8 Jenner of reality TV

DOWN

1 Say with a raised hand
2 "Pink Friday" rapper Minaj
3 Word repeated in "Ring Around the Rosie" before falling down
4 Google Maps function, briefly
6 "Shame on you!"

1	2	3	4	
5				
6				7
	8			
	9			

ACROSS

1 Reaction ___ (some Reddit posts)

5 The "E" of G.E.: Abbr.

6 "Wrecking Ball" singer Cyrus

8 Six-second looping video clip

9 Joe Jonas and Jake Gyllenhaal, to Taylor Swift

DOWN

1 Diamond or ruby

2 "___ for stuff like this"

3 Baumgarten who famously skydived from the stratosphere in 2014

4 Part of a movie

7 Cry with a fist pump

ACROSS

1 Sports bar array
4 Power, slangily
6 French "after"
7 ___ Carta
8 Foldaway bed

DOWN

1 Rapper with the 1996 nine-time platinum album "All Eyez on Me"
2 Sign between Leo and Libra
3 Bloodhound's trail
4 What a photocopier light may indicate
5 Spanish "that"

ACROSS

1 Valentine's Day symbol
5 Business for Shell or ExxonMobil
6 Valentine's Day symbol
8 Bill the Science Guy
9 Topless and bottomless

DOWN

1 Leonard who wrote "Hallelujah"
2 180-degree turn, slangily
3 Yoga pose that strengthens the abs
4 Was in a relationship with
7 Deli bread choice

1	2	3	■	4
5			6	
7				
8				
	■	9		

ACROSS

1 Homophone of 9-Across that shares no letters with it
5 "It's ___!" ("Easy-peasy!")
7 2008 Summer Olympics host
8 One who's jealous of your success
9 Homophone of 1-Across that shares no letters with it

DOWN

1 Millionaire's transport
2 Federal org. concerned with workplace injuries
3 Join forces
4 /, to a bowler
6 From square one

ACROSS

1 New Testament book
5 Cargo for UPS Airlines
6 Energetic (worth 21 points in Scrabble)
7 Numbers that never get smaller
8 Like the "Saw" films

DOWN

1 Pamplona pal
2 Bank heist, e.g.
3 A little drunk
4 On the ___ (furtively)
6 Sharp turn

	1	2	3	4
5				
6				
7				
8				

ACROSS

1 Place to play with a rubber duckie
5 Part of a computer's memory used for temporary data storage
6 "DJ Got Us Fallin' in Love" singer, 2010
7 Major ecological community
8 Gin flavoring

DOWN

1 Pizza herb
2 Sneeze sound
3 What every Sunday-Thursday NY Times crossword has
4 "___ goes nothing!"
5 Chicago team

ACROSS

1 6, written out
5 Sch. founded by Ben Franklin
7 Company that created Pong
8 Unacceptable
9 How many countries start with the letter "W"

DOWN

1 San ___ (capital of Puerto Rico)
2 "The Jungle" writer Sinclair
3 "Groovy!"
4 Energy giant that went bankrupt in 2001
6 Company that makes Air Jordans

	1	2	3	4
5				
6				
	■	7		
8				■

ACROSS

1 Wife of a 2-Down
5 Musical with the song "It's the Hard-Knock Life"
6 French school
7 TV screen choice, for short
8 Family ___

DOWN

1 "___ day now . . ."
2 Husband of a 1-Across
3 Daughter of a 2-Down
4 Prepared to hit, as a golf ball
5 Tons

	1	2	3	4
5				
6				
7				
8				

ACROSS

1 Prop on "The Bachelor"
5 "Aquí se ___ español"
   ("Spanish is spoken here")
6 Felix of "The Odd Couple"
7 Israel neighbor
8 Instrument in many a Daft
   Punk song

DOWN

1 Tall and long-limbed
2 Maternity ward doc
3 Snoozed
4 Google ___
5 Color tones

ACROSS

1 Snatch
4 Trojan War beauty
6 Evil Queen's offering to Snow White
7 Company that owned Tumblr until 2017
8 Field with cases and briefs

DOWN

1 Himalayan country
2 Leader of the pack
3 Word before zero or average
4 Horse power?
5 Movie character that dodged bullets in slow motion

36

ACROSS

1 Soccer star Suarez
5 Henry VIII's second or fourth wife
6 "Indubitably!"
7 Block in Washington
8 Rapper's group

DOWN

1 Matt of "The Today Show"
2 Band together
3 Following behind, as a broken-down car
4 "What'd I tell you?"
6 TV shopper's channel

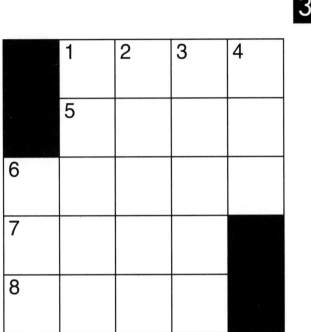

ACROSS

1 Voting nay
5 "Better Call ____," spin-off of "Breaking Bad"
6 Dancing animal in Katy Perry's Super Bowl halftime show
7 "What the ____!"
8 First-class org.?

DOWN

1 Remains by the fire
2 Org. co-founded by W. E. B. Du Bois
3 Istanbul natives
4 Type
6 Moo ____ beef

38

1	2	3	4	
5				
6				7
	8			
	9			

ACROSS

1 Impulsive
5 ___ Blacc, singer with the 2014 hit "The Man"
6 Internet award
8 Make over completely
9 Jeff Bridges sci-fi classic

DOWN

1 Like sashimi and steak tartare
2 Wide awake
3 Like the designated driver, hopefully
4 French magazine Charlie ___
7 Over there, poetically

ACROSS

1 One of journalism's five W's
4 One of journalism's five W's
5 Piles
7 Fiery passion
8 Midterms and finals

DOWN

1 One of journalism's five W's
2 Coin toss call
3 Baked, so to speak
4 One of journalism's five W's
6 Sophs., in two years

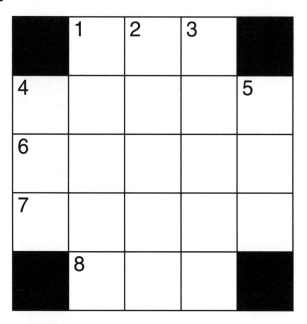

ACROSS

1 Dumbbell abbr.
4 Raccoon relative
6 Subject of a donor card
7 Demolish
8 Antlered animal

DOWN

1 Chuck who created "The Big Bang Theory" and "Mom"
2 Well-rounded breakfast?
3 Poker chip collection
4 Animal on Wisconsin's quarter
5 Tattoos, slangily

1	2	3	4	■
5				■
6				7
8				
9				

ACROSS

1 Dove soap shape
5 Talking iPhone feature
6 MTV house-touring show
8 New ___ (modern spiritualists)
9 Some Spanish flowers

DOWN

1 "And the ___ goes to . . ."
2 August 23–September 21
3 March 21–April 20
4 September 22–October 23
7 Leaky tire sound

ACROSS

1 Watch sound
5 High-end Honda division
7 Feature of Oregon sales
8 Butter cutter
9 Adjusts, as an alarm clock

DOWN

1 In the ____ (performing poorly)
2 iPhone screen array
3 Sweetie pie
4 Maker of Kool-Aid, Jell-O and Miracle Whip
6 x and y, on a graph

	1	2	3	4
5				
6				
7				
8				

ACROSS

1 Vending machine choice
5 ___ Wars (Rome vs. Carthage conflicts)
6 Make amends
7 Some boxing punches
8 "Sharknado" channel

DOWN

1 Adorable sort
2 Wall switch words
3 Like a dryer trap
4 Top poker pair
5 Best buds

44

	1	2	3	4
5				
6				
7				
8				■

ACROSS

1 "Frozen" character with an ice palace
5 Makes beer
6 Queen ___ lace
7 "Frantic ___ Searching Dog Shelter for Bo Look-Alike" ("The Onion" headline)
8 App with restaurant reviews

DOWN

1 "Sesame Street" resident
2 #1 tennis player for much of the '80s
3 Remove dust bunnies
4 Part of N.R.A.: Abbr.
5 Justin Bieber song whose video has the most dislikes in YouTube history

ACROSS

1 Make small talk
5 Shower drain clogger
6 Covered with a thin layer, as eyes
7 Shelfmate of Vogue
8 Ran out of juice

DOWN

1 Tailgating dish
2 Berry of "Catwoman"
3 Aligned the cross hairs
4 "___ not to laugh . . ."
6 Monetary policy group, with "the"

46

ACROSS

1 Too-good-to-be-true investment
5 Laker legend, familiarly
6 Touch and shuffle
8 See 1-Down
9 ___ Puft Marshmallow Man, "Ghostbusters" character

DOWN

1 With 8-Across, winter break getaway
2 Egyptian Christians
3 End prematurely
4 Journalists, collectively
7 Only Stratego piece with a letter on it

ACROSS

1 ____ Levine, lead singer of Maroon 5
5 Common cat food flavor
6 Kelly of NBC News
8 Highchair component
9 ____ in progress (iPhone phrase)

DOWN

1 Target of thieves who do card skimming
2 Many performances at the Grammys
3 Steamed
4 Like some ancient pyramids
7 One side of the GW Bridge

ACROSS

1 It gets flatter as it gets older
5 Like many intramural sports leagues
6 Ancient Incan capital
7 Competitor of Lyft
8 "___ there, tiger!"

DOWN

1 ___ diving (tropical vacation activity)
2 Moves like honey
3 Criticize sharply
4 Commotion
6 Pool ball striker

ACROSS

1 N.Y.C. airport
4 All worked up
6 Now, in Spain
7 Alternative to "The Jerry Springer Show"
8 Like some martinis

DOWN

1 Islamic holy war
2 What many gluten-free recipes lack
3 ___ Washington, star of ABC's "Scandal"
4 Bump in bumper cars, maybe
5 Something that breaks every morning?

ACROSS

1 "Hang on, putting my phone down a sec"
4 Comparative with ice
6 Comparative with mud
8 Comparative with pie
9 Word often ignored when alphabetizing

DOWN

1 Include secretly on an email
2 The "R" of gaming's RPG
3 Sheep's cry
5 Sprint
7 Kind of whiskey

ACROSS

1 "Wheel of Fortune" action
5 Children's TV character who's the only non-human to testify before Congress
6 Image on the back of a quarter
8 When asked if her husband had a hobby, Mary Todd Lincoln replied "___"
9 Baby blues, e.g.

DOWN

1 "___ what I'm sayin?"
2 Park ___ (Monopoly property)
3 Coming out phrase
4 Nick of "48 Hrs."
7 Tricky road bend

52

	1	2	3	4
5				
6				
7				
8				

ACROSS

1 Beyond the ____
(unacceptable)
5 With 7-Across, axiom about
wealth's influence
6 Swimming pool concern
7 See 5-Across
8 Mucho : Spanish ::
____ : French

DOWN

1 ____ vortex, winter weather
phenomenon
2 It's measured in degrees
3 Unauthorized disclosures
4 Features of potatoes . . . and
Mr. Potato Head
5 LeBlanc of "Friends"

1	**2**	**3**	■		
4			**5**	**6**	
7					
■	**8**				
■	**9**				

ACROSS

1 "____ be my pleasure"
4 "Say Yes to the ___":
TLC reality show
7 "The Metamorphosis" author
8 Genre for Otis Redding and
Sam Cooke
9 NBA champions in 2012
and 2013

DOWN

1 "No idea," in text messages
2 Place to drag old files
3 "Robinson Crusoe" author
5 Arctic seabird
6 Pretzel topper

ACROSS

1 Arizona city east of Phoenix
5 The Earth turns on it
6 See 6-Down
7 Ready and willing partner
8 Homer's hangout on "The Simpsons"

DOWN

1 Cuban dance
2 Napoleon on Elba, e.g.
3 Rotten Tomatoes and Jezebel
4 Something an e-cigarette lacks
6 With 6-Across, winner of four Grammys at the 2015 Grammy Awards

1	2	3	4	
5				6
7				
8				
	9			

ACROSS

1 Uncertain
5 Openings mentioned in Neutrogena ads
7 Prolonged suffering
8 Checks for fingerprints
9 Russell Simmons' clothing line ___ Farm

DOWN

1 Apple product
2 Get steamy, as a window
3 First-year student, informally
4 Gossipy sort
6 The "S" in GPS: Abbr.

	1	2	3	4
	5			
6				
7				
8				

ACROSS

1 Wilts
5 Unit of currency in the Harry Potter books
6 3/14, to a math lover
7 Prince Charles, for the British throne
8 Carded at a club

DOWN

1 Enjoyed Aspen
2 MacDowell of "Groundhog Day"
3 Basketball position
4 Pig pen
6 ____ Beta Kappa

ACROSS

1 With 8-Across, high-
definition photos of cake
or bacon, e.g.
5 River to the Rhine
6 "Here, I'll do that"
7 Brainstorm
8 See 1-Across

DOWN

1 Corleone brother who broke
Michael's heart
2 North Carolina's ____ Banks
3 "Whew, that's tough!"
4 Anthony Anderson's character
on ABC's "Black-ish"
6 Place for ChapStick

ACROSS

1 "Don't worry about me"
5 Kaplan who played Kotter on "Welcome Back, Kotter"
6 Predator's opponent, in the movies
7 Snug
8 There are five per foot

DOWN

1 White house?
2 Indian corn
3 Does as told
4 Jennings who won 74 times in a row on "Jeopardy!"
6 Affordable Care ____

	1	2	3	4
5				
6				
7				
8				

ACROSS

1 Stereotypical dog name
5 Guys who make people look good
6 With 7-Across, what C and D indicate on boarding passes
7 See 6-Across
8 Bookies give them

DOWN

1 Mentally exhausted
2 :-(
3 Shoulder muscles
4 White bills in Monopoly
5 El ___, Texas

1	2	3	4	5
6				
7				
8				
9				

ACROSS

1 Country that's nearly 25 times as long as its average width
6 Tryst participant
7 Pissed off
8 "The Rachel Maddow Show" carrier
9 Attack on all sides

DOWN

1 Scale, as a mountain
2 Chess knight, essentially
3 Several Russian czars
4 Leave alone
5 Standing upright

1	2	3	4	■
5				■
6				7
■	8			
■	9			

ACROSS

1 Condition treated with Adderall, in brief
5 Dutch South African
6 ♠
8 Goofs
9 Resign, with "down"

DOWN

1 Gym regular's pride
2 Takes steroids
3 ♥
4 Rapper who co-founded Death Row Records
7 Paranormal power, for short

ACROSS

1 Not a permanent employee
5 2009 Wimbledon semifinalist Tommy
6 Cartoon mouse
7 Skinny swimmers
8 See 6-Down

DOWN

1 Org. headquartered in Brussels
2 Some London lords
3 Heron habitat
4 "Gangnam Style" singer
6 With 8-Across, 2016 presidential hopeful

1	2	3	4	5
6				
7				
8				
9				

ACROSS

1 Essentials
6 Two cents' worth
7 One place to find sweaters
8 Bird that's the symbol of the National Audubon Society
9 Cycle after wash

DOWN

1 Penny pincher
2 Eel, at a sushi restaurant
3 Reject with disdain
4 Things to whistle
5 John Kerry's department

ACROSS

1 "Aww, ___!" ("Oh no he didn't!")
5 Bedsheet's use at a frat party
6 "Over my dead body!"
7 Fifty-fifty
8 Mark from a whipping

DOWN

1 Jobs in the tech industry
2 "White Teeth" or "Black Beauty"
3 State Farm employee
4 Golf standard
6 Part of four state names

ACROSS

1 ___ chi: Chinese martial art
4 With 6- and 8-Across, suddenly become famous
6 See 4-Across
7 Xbox competitor
8 See 4-Across

DOWN

1 Garment of ancient Greece
2 "Glee" character in a wheelchair
3 -like equivalent
4 Weapons for Katniss Everdeen and Legolas
5 Prefix with -prompter or -port

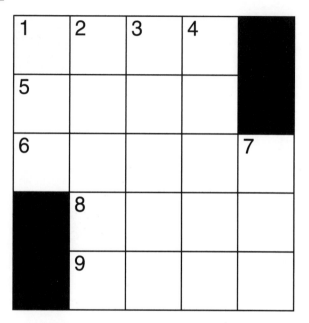

ACROSS

1 Luxury car brand, informally
5 Color that's Latin for "water"
6 ___ pricing: Uber tactic
8 "Make it snappy!"
9 "___ try that again"

DOWN

1 English majors' degs.
2 Splenda competitor
3 Carla on "Scrubs," e.g.
4 Big name in restaurant ratings
7 Mini-albums, briefly

	T	I	P	
T	O	R	I	C
S	W	E	A	R
P	E	N	N	Y
	L	E	O	

ACROSS

1 15%–20%, for a waiter
4 Doughnut-shaped
6 Use cusswords
7 What has a head, a tail, is brown, and has no legs?
8 Zodiac lion

DOWN

1 What gets wetter as it dries?
2 2000 comedy "Me, Myself & ___"
3 What has keys that don't unlock anything?
4 Small amt. in baking
5 Shed tears

68

ACROSS

1 Places where masseurs massage
5 Victoria's Secret lingerie line
6 Dark and dreary
7 The "a" in a.m.
8 The "15" of 3/26/15

DOWN

1 Place for a book title
2 In 1492 it sailed the ocean blue
3 Rile up
4 Chicken Little's concern
6 The "26" of 3/26/15

	1	2	3	4
5				
6				
7				
8				

ACROSS

1 Hockey disk
5 Home of the Burj Khalifa, the world's tallest building
6 They have their own newspaper page
7 Travelocity.com info
8 Suffix with Oktober

DOWN

1 Cocoon occupants
2 Modern alternatives to cabs
3 Military academy enrollee
4 The "x" of the letter sign-off xoxo
5 Remove, as a hat

ACROSS

1 Sleepover attire, for short
4 Animal life
6 Burger topper
7 Burger topper
8 Convened

DOWN

1 One-time international airline
2 Beverage in a box
3 High-and-mighty type
4 Pocket watch accessory
5 ___ Arbor, Mich.

ACROSS

1 "Yeah, like that's gonna happen"
5 Chris who played Captain Kirk in 2009's "Star Trek"
6 Eccentric
7 Crafts material in a stick
8 Squarish

DOWN

1 Olympic speed skater Ohno
2 ___ Falls (largest city in South Dakota)
3 Harmonizing with the group
4 Tina who co-created Netflix's "Unbreakable Kimmy Schmidt"
6 C.I.A. Cold War counterpart

72

ACROSS

1 X-rated stuff
5 Italian city that's home to "The Last Supper"
7 Loosen, as shoelaces
8 HBO show
9 Get cheeky with

DOWN

1 Quite pleased with oneself
2 BMW models featured in "The Italian Job"
3 Prefix with sonic or violet
4 Flip comment?
6 Loch ___ monster

	1	2	3	4
	5			
6				
7				
8				

ACROSS

1 Programming language that's also the name of an island
5 Event depicted in "Saving Private Ryan"
6 2008 Pixar robot
7 End in ___ (finish evenly)
8 Unpaid credit card bills, e.g.

DOWN

1 Online service for Jewish singles
2 Wing it on stage
3 Restaurant worker who's rarely in the restaurant
4 Affirmative vote
6 Roll of banknotes

	1	2	3	4
5				
6				
7				
8				

ACROSS

1 German currency replaced by the euro
5 Get clean
6 Like the sun after dawn
7 The J. and K. in J.K. Rowling, e.g.: Abbr.
8 Message with an emoji, maybe

DOWN

1 Its state flag has a moose on it
2 When a happy hour might start
3 Butler of "Gone With the Wind"
4 Big name in salad dressing
5 One Direction's Liam or Harry, e.g.

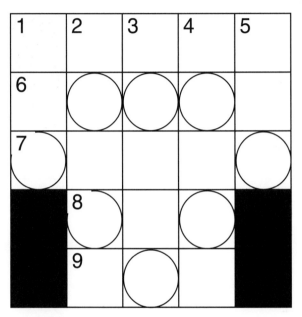

ACROSS

1 What many pro wrestling broadcasts are
6 American ____ (U.S. territory)
7 Cuzco resident, once
8 Father
9 Letter before tee

DOWN

1 Pitchfork-shaped Greek letter
2 "Duck Dynasty" channel
3 Community rec centers
4 Relatives of frogs
5 Many an airport shuttle

ACROSS

1 Adidas competitor
5 Latin word on a penny
6 Means of connection
8 Fancy-schmancy
9 "South Park" co-creator Parker

DOWN

1 Band with the 2012 #1 hit "We Are Young"
2 Like a butterfingers
3 Vegas hotel shaped like a pyramid
4 Cause to chuckle
7 Like a wallflower

	1	2	3	4
5				
6				
7				
8				

ACROSS

1 When repeated, a Hawaiian food fish
5 Part of Great Britain
6 Spin around
7 Volkswagen model since 1979
8 Physician with a daily talk show

DOWN

1 HBO's "Real Time With Bill ___"
2 Supreme Court justice Samuel
3 Avis competitor
4 Land surrounded by agua
5 Christian bracelet letters

1	2	3	4	5
6				
7				
8				
9				

ACROSS

1 Change with the times
6 With 7-Across, holder of symbolic foods on Passover
7 See 6-Across
8 Shark-filming precautions
9 Bill ____, controversial figure in the 2008 presidential election

DOWN

1 Pet welfare org.
2 Rain's effect on a baseball game
3 "A watched pot never boils," e.g.
4 Dinklage who plays Tyrion Lannister on "Game of Thrones"
5 Lock of hair

1	2	3	4	
5				6
7				
8				
	9			

ACROSS

1 Amenity at a coffee shop or airport
5 Draw forth
7 Cassette half
8 Roman garments
9 Phantom ___ (imagined phone vibration)

DOWN

1 Opposite of 6-Down, on a map
2 Moron
3 Rich chocolate treat
4 Glacier climber's tool
6 Opposite of 1-Down, on a map

80

	1	2	3	4
	5			
6				
7				
8				

ACROSS

1 iPhone buys
5 Pan handler?
6 Managed to survive
7 "For here ___ go?"
8 Jet-black gem

DOWN

1 Desire of the squirrel in "Ice Age"
2 ___ mouth (one using foul language)
3 Part of many a business address: Abbr.
4 Big ___ (phrase on Montana license plates)
6 Sticky stuff

ACROSS

1 F.B.I. employee: Abbr.
4 Hit the dirt, in baseball
7 Baseball highlight
8 Wang of fashion
9 Causes of colds

DOWN

1 Baseball bat wood
2 Baseball gear
3 Boggle game need
5 Skin: Suffix
6 Baseball pitching stats

ACROSS

1 Bearded African animal
4 The "D" of F.D.A.
5 Ministry of ____, in Orwell's "1984"
6 Fridge sounds
7 Official behind a catcher

DOWN

1 Curmudgeon
2 Items in a squirrel's stash
3 "I'm so over all this"
4 A rock band's name often appears on it
5 Day "Scandal" airs: Abbr.

83

	1	2	3	4
5				
6				
7				
8				

ACROSS

1 Have to have
5 Saab competitor
6 Room at the top
7 Artist's cover-up
8 Shelters near a campfire

DOWN

1 "Musta been someone else!"
2 John who sang "Rocket Man"
3 Force out, as from an apartment
4 Waterfront worksites
5 Far-reaching

ACROSS

1 Dollar parts: Abbr.
4 Koenig who hosted the Serial podcast
6 Caribbean resort island
7 Another name for the drug ecstasy
8 Top seed's reward

DOWN

1 Chocolate substitute
2 Yours ____
3 Expensive fur
4 ____ Seaborn, Rob Lowe's character on "The West Wing"
5 What pitchforks pitch

ACROSS

1 Rating for many "Seinfeld" episodes

5 One sleeping "in the jungle, the mighty jungle," in song

6 Hour and minute separator

8 New ewe

9 Region

DOWN

1 Special attention for a patient, in brief

2 String quartet member

3 Opposite of equatorial

4 Pointy-hatted garden figure

7 Org. that annually gives the Sixth Man Award

86

ACROSS

1 Tobacco-free nicotine product, informally
5 ____ Day (April holiday)
7 "Spider-Man" director Sam
8 S and M, on clothing tags
9 Long look

DOWN

1 What friends, Romans and countrymen lent, in Shakespeare
2 Daniel who plays James Bond
3 Spanish resort island
4 Selena of "Spring Breakers"
6 Opposite of fall

	1	2	3
4	5		
6			
7			
8			

ACROSS

1 Paintballer's need
4 Home to the N.F.L.'s Dolphins
6 Indo-European
7 Squiggly line in piñata
8 NNW's opposite

DOWN

1 Oprah's best friend
2 "___ bro?" (internet meme that mocks your anger)
3 First digit in a California ZIP code
4 Yoga studio equipment
5 Colored part of the eye

ACROSS

1 Rocker whose "Morning Phase" won the 2015 Album of the Year

5 Imperative from Mr. Miyagi of "The Karate Kid"

6 Kevin Hart, for the Comedy Central roast of Justin Bieber

7 Place to live

8 Features of fashionable jeans

DOWN

1 Thumper's "deer friend"

2 Former police officer

3 Female college students, quaintly

4 Patella's place

5 Have on

1	2	3		4
5			■	
6			7	
	■	8		
9				

ACROSS

1 Corporate regulation
5 Daniels who directed "The Butler"
6 Big name in arcade games
8 Animal in a maze
9 Rapper who said "I am Shakespeare in the flesh"

DOWN

1 Like some crossword squares
2 To this point
3 Live and ____
4 Like some crossword squares
7 "____ Donovan": Showtime drama

90

ACROSS

1 ___ ed requirements
4 Italian salami city
6 Green-skinned pear
7 Northernmost N.Y.C. borough
8 Peacock tail feature

DOWN

1 Comedy or horror
2 Waiter's parting word after serving
3 Who opposed George Washington for president in 1792
4 Shoot the breeze
5 ___ cable (TV hookup)

	1	2	3	4
5				
6				
7				
8				

ACROSS

1 Setting for much of "Back to the Future"
5 Most U.S. states have a Latin one
6 ___.com, popular question-answering site
7 Four-time NBA All-Star Rajon ___
8 Former flames

DOWN

1 Rented U.S. mail receptacle
2 Make up (for)
3 Handsome hunks
4 1970s–'80s rock band with a repetitive name
5 Filly's mother

	1	2	3	
4				5
6				
7				
8				

ACROSS

1 Yosemite ____, Looney Tunes character
4 8-Across on the Lebanese flag
6 Lunch time, for some
7 Reclines lazily
8 See 4-Across and 3-Down

DOWN

1 Mister in Mexico
2 "Rolling in the Deep" singer
3 8-Across that's a symbol of Canada
4 Stallion-to-be
5 Apt. units

1	2	3	4	
5				6
7				
8				
	9			

ACROSS

1 ____ hands
5 Look forward to
7 Color of many bras
8 Twilled fabric used for making suits
9 The Black ____, Grammy-winning rockers

DOWN

1 Quick punches
2 Every seven days
3 Congo, from 1971 to 1997
4 Big-nosed comics character with lots of pets
6 Equipment golfers use that miniature golfers don't

	1	2	3	4
5				
6				
7				
8				

ACROSS

1 Werewolf film sound
5 Rescuer of Princess Peach
6 "___ is never without a reason, but seldom with a good one": Benjamin Franklin
7 Dahl who wrote "Charlie and the Chocolate Factory"
8 Compassionate

DOWN

1 Vietnam's capital
2 Heart or kidney
3 Exercise, as power
4 Title for Voldemort
5 Word following question or quotation

ACROSS

1 Chess knight, to some
5 Picasso's ___ Period, 1901–04
6 Like some bodybuilders' bodies
8 The "V" of V.I.P.
9 Section of a hip-hop song

DOWN

1 "Last Week Tonight With John Oliver" airer
2 Martini garnish
3 King or queen
4 Crystal ball users
7 Easter egg coloring

ACROSS

1 Custardy Spanish dessert
4 Crusty dessert
5 Many a dance club song
7 Halloween mo.
8 Eat dessert, e.g.

DOWN

1 "Fee, ____, foe, fum"
2 ____ meringue (kind of 4-Across)
3 In the on-deck circle
4 Cattle poker
6 ____ cream

ACROSS

1 The 2% in 2% milk
4 Place for a patch on a suit
6 Word in two U.S. state names
7 Actress Parker
8 Obama or Clinton, briefly

DOWN

1 Natural disaster in Genesis
2 Treat poorly
3 Emblem carved on a pole
4 Mind reader's ability, briefly
5 Kid's repeated question

ACROSS

1 Home to Zion National Park
5 Fight the power
7 Choking on a Life Saver, e.g.
8 Give the cold shoulder
9 Waterway between Earth and Hades

DOWN

1 "Exodus" novelist (whose name is an anagram of a Cruise kid)
2 University of Maryland athletes, informally
3 "It's ___ time!"
4 "Give me liberty or give me death!" speaker
6 Bobcat cousin

	1	2	3	4
	5			
6				
7				
8				

ACROSS

1 Sudden impulse
5 Give 1 out of 5 stars, say
6 "What a guy!"
7 Mrs. George Clooney
8 Refuse

DOWN

1 "What did I do to deserve this?"
2 Villain in the Jewish holiday of Purim
3 Europe's "boot"
4 See 6-Down
6 With 4-Down, cable drama about Don Draper

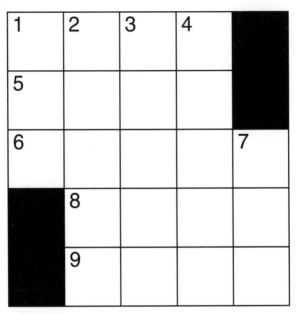

ACROSS

1 Guitar legend Hendrix
5 Member of Bush's "axis of evil"
6 Monopoly railroad
8 ___ pro quo
9 Kindle Fire competitor

DOWN

1 Triangular sail
2 Baghdad dad, for example
3 "Stop being such a wimp!"
4 Columbus's intended destination
7 "Hmm, that's ___"

1	**2**	**3**	**4**	**5**
6				
7				
■	**8**			
9				■

ACROSS

1 Own up to
6 An elephant, a car, a tree
7 Rodeo rope
8 Fight between families
9 A wine glass, a cherry, a rose

DOWN

1 The "A" in NATO: Abbr.
2 A paper, the military, an open window
3 What the Louvre is, to a Parisian
4 "To recap . . ."
5 Eliminated from a boxing match

ACROSS

1 Word before "you're it"
4 It's all ears?
5 Tourney winner
6 Name on toy fuel trucks
7 Abbr. after a telephone number

DOWN

1 Part of a square meal?
2 ___ race
3 Econ. yardstick
4 Part of a square meal?
5 ___ Guevara

ACROSS

1 Lose, as a big lead
5 Class instructor, informally
6 Where hurricanes originate
7 Swindle
8 Fork-tailed flier

DOWN

1 "You ___ judge"
2 PowerPoint pointer
3 Its floor is always wet
4 Word from the hard-of-hearing
5 Saying "I'm not sure that dress looks perfect on you," e.g.

ACROSS

1 The "m" of e=mc^2
5 Fertility clinic cell
6 Site of a massive 2015 earthquake
8 ___ Aslan, academic known for a viral 2013 Fox News interview
9 Creature on the cover of "Jurassic Park"

DOWN

1 When M.L.K. Day is celebrated: Abbr.
2 Keep from happening
3 "Fantastic!"
4 Urban air problem
7 Far from strict

ACROSS

1 Weight on one's shoulders
5 Wall Street math expert, informally
6 Horseshoe-shaped lab item that sounds like a popular website
7 Symbol on a "This way" sign
8 Paris pair

DOWN

1 Bizarre
2 Pacific island nation
3 Take out of the packaging
4 Crock-Pot potful
5 College campus focal point

ACROSS

1 "Don't touch that ___!"
5 Jargon
6 Choice words
7 Home to Bates College
8 Zebras and gnus, to lions

DOWN

1 Iraqi currency
2 The movie "Boyhood," e.g.
3 Hellish suffering
4 The stuff of legends
5 Reading light

ACROSS

1 Utterance after sinking into a hot bath
4 ____ Mayweather, boxing opponent of 7-Across
6 HBO, for "Game of Thrones"
7 ____ Pacquiao, boxing opponent of 4-Across
8 Word before cow, horse, or lion

DOWN

1 Name after "a.k.a."
2 Singer Lena or Marilyn
3 Villainous animal in "The Lion King"
4 Relatives, slangily
5 Having little rainfall

ACROSS

1 Cluck of disapproval
4 Greetings from pirates
6 Animal voiced by George Clooney in a Wes Anderson film
7 Checkroom garments
8 Eye liner?

DOWN

1 Pulsate painfully
2 Up to this point
3 _____ Protocol: UN global-warming agreement
4 "The Walking Dead" channel
5 Annual festival in Austin, Tx., familiarly

ACROSS

1 Reason for an air quality alert
5 Do some roadwork
6 Element of many a Snapchat story
7 "___ hardly wait!"
8 Rival businesses in "Dodgeball: A True Underdog Story"

DOWN

1 Getting five alarms, on a menu
2 ___ Speaker
3 Kitchen appliances
4 Prefix with thermal
6 Percent deducted from a gambler's winnings by the casino

ACROSS

1 Popular EA Sports game
5 Two or three
6 Kitchen appliance
7 Powerful wind
8 Abbr. at the end of a long internet comment

DOWN

1 Deadly
2 Words of resignation at the poker table
3 High temperature
4 Shock and ___
6 Rank for former Taliban prisoner Bowe Bergdahl: Abbr.

1	2	3	4	5
6				
7				
8				
9				

ACROSS

1 Brand of ibuprofen
6 Google ___ (cloud storage space)
7 Audacity
8 "___ Your Love" (2013 hit for Calvin Harris and Ellie Goulding)
9 Works the bar

DOWN

1 ___ one (ticket phrase)
2 Vehicle for the C.I.A.'s Special Activities Division
3 One of Santa's reindeer
4 Like the outfield walls at Wrigley Field
5 English city NE of Manchester

ACROSS
1 The "D" of D.J.
5 "Stop trying to make ____ happen" (oft-quoted "Mean Girls" line)
6 Pond scum
7 Driver's reversal
8 Dissenting votes

DOWN
1 Airline with a triangle logo
2 One providing assistance after a crash
3 Surgery marks
4 Julie ____, host of TV's "Big Brother"
5 Mr. Tumnus, in "The Chronicles of Narnia"

	1	2	3	
4				5
6				
7				
	8			

ACROSS

1 "The Boy Next Door" star, familiarly
4 Mickey Mouse's friend
6 Mickey Mouse's pet
7 "Men in Black" creature
8 Currency whose symbol is a "Y" with two horizontal lines through it

DOWN

1 Like the Green Giant
2 FX series frequently set in the Comedy Cellar
3 On more than one occasion
4 No. between 0 and 4
5 Over there, poetically

ACROSS

1 Emails with fake subject lines
5 Tilt toward the sky
7 Crowd scene actor
8 Colorful violet
9 Masses of fish eggs

DOWN

1 Instruction manual segment
2 Animation studio with the film "Inside Out"
3 5A, for Jerry on "Seinfeld": Abbr.
4 Portmanteau for a fashion-forward men's accessory
6 Uses Venmo, say

ACROSS

1 Response to a poker bet
4 Napoleon or Snowball, in "Animal Farm"
5 Response to a poker bet
7 Shower curtain suspender
8 Response to a poker bet

DOWN

1 World Factbook publisher, in brief
2 "I Kissed ___": Katy Perry hit
3 Told a whopper
4 Grad student's mentor
6 Landscaper's purchase

ACROSS

1 Word after laughing or natural

4 2008 title role for Adam Sandler

6 Takes off like a rocket

7 Trendy dance fitness program

8 4:00 English drink

DOWN

1 Hit the town

2 "Oh, give me _____ . . ."

3 Brazilian dance

4 Snoring, in comics

5 Govt. org. whose logo depicts an eagle standing on a key

ACROSS

1 Canadian ___ (food)
4 Dutch ___ (meal)
7 French ___ (food)
8 Veer off the beaten path

DOWN

1 Ashtray accumulation
2 E.M.T.'s cry before using a defibrillator
3 Kooky
5 Problem in old wood
6 Happy ___ clam

ACROSS

1 H.O.V. lane user
4 Most Monopoly properties have six different ones
6 The M of M.L.B.
7 Battle mementos
8 "That's a stumper . . ."

DOWN

1 Lifeguard's workplace
2 Fix, as a photocopier
3 Weather Channel concern
4 Apartment ad abbreviation
5 Most AARP members: Abbr.

ACROSS

1 Toxic pollutant banned since the 1970s
4 Crucial artery
7 Patrol for prey
8 Celebrity photographer Leibovitz
9 Turkey, to a bowler

DOWN

1 "____ Don't Preach" (Madonna hit)
2 Ears that can't hear
3 Yankee Stadium locale
5 "Need a moment? Chew it over with ____" (ad slogan)
6 Women's soccer star Morgan

ACROSS

1 Twitter, Facebook and Instagram
5 Certain Starbucks order, informally
6 *prayer hands emoji*
7 "___ chance!"
8 Marlboro alternative

DOWN

1 Sound muffled by a handkerchief
2 Snapshot
3 Of the Vatican
4 You, in German
6 What print books have that Kindles don't

121

ACROSS

1 Federal health agcy.

4 Tire pattern

6 Pleasant, weatherwise

7 What Tinder users and petty thieves both do

8 What Shakespeare and football teams both have

DOWN

1 What pubgoers and babies both do

2 Novelist/screenwriter Ephron

3 Amusingly outlandish

4 Recipe amt.

5 Hair colorers

ACROSS

1 Jackson 5 #1 hit of 1970
4 Give a hard time
6 N.Y.C. country club?
8 Grp. defending individual rights
9 Shelter with a thatch roof, maybe

DOWN

1 Performance ____
2 ____ Men ("Who Let the Dogs Out" group)
3 Prague native
5 South African tribesman
7 Item in a squirrel's stash

ACROSS

1 Pops in the microwave
5 Land on the Sea of Japan
6 Circular space shuttle gasket
7 Origami bird
8 "___ smokes!"

DOWN

1 Hero with a trademark "Z"
2 Standard Windows typeface
3 Coin for a gumball machine
4 Wise guy?
5 ___ Brothers (influential Republican donors)

	1	2	3	
4				5
6				
7				
8				

ACROSS

1 Merchandise: Abbr.
4 Posting on Instagram
6 Beard remover
7 NBC newsman Roger
8 2014 #1 hit for Iggy Azalea

DOWN

1 Loser to the U.S. in the 2014 World Cup
2 Egg carton count
3 Uncomplaining in the face of adversity
4 Univ. employee
5 Paris airport

1	**2**	**3**	**4**	**5**
6				
7				
8				
9				

ACROSS

1 Attach with needle and thread
6 Cat's instrument in a classic viral video
7 Nixon's first vice president
8 ___ circus
9 Texter's "for real?!"

DOWN

1 Bombards with junk email
2 Much-climbed peak in the Bernese Alps
3 Purchases at Ollivanders in the Harry Potter books
4 Buck ___, first African-American coach in Major League Baseball
5 "Not a chance!"

ACROSS

1 Vegas's ___ Grand
4 Bounce off the walls
6 By oneself
7 "Arrested Development" surname
8 2015 Melissa McCarthy movie

DOWN

1 Crowded places on Black Friday
2 Word before discussion or dynamics
3 ___ Python
4 Vehicle from the airport
5 "It was . . . just ok"

1		**2**	**3**	**4**
	■	**5**		
6	**7**			
8			■	
9				

ACROSS

1 ___ bear (gray)
5 Gen ___ (baby boomer's successor)
6 ___ bear (white)
8 French article
9 ___ bear (brown)

DOWN

1 Completely dead
2 Connected, as car wheels
3 Open grassy area
4 Table of data, e.g.
7 First number dialed when calling long distance

	1	2	3	4
	5			
6				
7				
8				

ACROSS

1 Mall tenant
5 ____ de France
6 Like a sullen child
7 Behind, in Britspeak
8 Dandelion or crabgrass

DOWN

1 Mall tenant
2 Nancy Pelosi's place of work, with "the"
3 No longer in the closet, say
4 Inquire about private matters
6 Pussy foot?

ACROSS

1 Money for the poor
5 Rise
6 Handicapped character on "South Park"
7 Noise in a comic book gunfight
8 Say no to

DOWN

1 Nimble
2 Willy _____, the salesman in "Death of a Salesman"
3 Q: Why was the _____ so tense? A: He was all wound up
4 Austin Powers or James Bond
6 Awaiting scheduling: Abbr.

1	2	3	4	5
6				
7				
■	8			
■	■	9		

ACROSS

1 "Are not!" retort
6 Protector of the ___ (title in "Game of Thrones")
7 ___ Antoinette
8 Justin of "Dodgeball"
9 Lipton product

DOWN

1 Where the humerus bone is
2 Purchase from Seamless.com
3 Set of fortunetelling cards
4 Quarterback protectors, in football slang
5 Greek letter used as a symbol for ohms

ACROSS

1 "I get it now!"
4 "Robinson Crusoe" author
6 "The Hitchhiker's Guide to the Galaxy" author
7 Winter Olympic sleds
8 Before, poetically

DOWN

1 No longer a minor
2 "Iliad" author
3 "Siddhartha" author
4 The N.F.L.'s Cowboys, on scoreboards
5 www.harvard.___

1	**2**	**3**	**4**	**5**
6				
7				
8				
9				

ACROSS

1 Depicts unfairly, as data
6 Diet with a lot of berries, meat and nuts
7 Liam Neeson voices him in the "Narnia" films
8 Hindu god called "the destroyer"
9 Stingy sort

DOWN

1 Involuntary twitch
2 Whole-grain cereal brand
3 Bret Easton ____, "American Psycho" novelist
4 Construct, as an elaborate lie
5 Dolphins use it to find fish

ACROSS

1 Place for an unhatched chick
4 → Greek god ← Egyptian port
5 → Kind of wafer ← Certain poker bet
6 → Dance move ← Cats and dogs
7 ___ ball (terrible basketball shot)

DOWN

1 Conger catcher
2 ↓ Big swallow ↑ Advertisement
3 Fed. property agency
4 Baked Italian entree
5 Secretive org.

ACROSS

1 "Hang on a sec . . . ," in text messages
4 "We Will Rock You" band
6 "Survivor" faction
7 Informal "See what I mean?"
8 Egyptian snake

DOWN

1 Garment worn by some Muslim women
2 Carriage driver's controls
3 Jazz style
4 Amt.
5 Like iPods in 2001

	1	2	3	4
5				
6				
7				
8				

ACROSS

1 Mound
5 2015 Will Smith film
6 "I was at home when the crime occurred," e.g.
7 ___ notes (CD insert)
8 Fireplace fuel

DOWN

1 F.D.R. affliction
2 Sweetest part of a cake
3 Applies oil to
4 Ascend (entered appropriately in this grid)
5 Plummet (entered appropriately in this grid)

136

	1	2	3	4
	5			
6				
7				
8				

ACROSS

1 Title in an Uncle Remus story
5 First name in jeans
6 Team ___ ("Twilight" fan group)
7 "Don't worry about me"
8 There's one for curly hair

DOWN

1 Point the finger at
2 Scout's job, briefly
3 Bring to mind
4 Word before cage or eye
6 "The ___ is up!"

	1	2	3	4
5				
6				
7				
8				

ACROSS

1 Word after sweet, soft or sun
5 Carried
6 Cream of the crop
7 Marge Simpson or Lois Griffin
8 ___ Blatter, former head of FIFA

DOWN

1 Finish, as a crossword
2 Prepare to go out
3 Good way to go out
4 Abound (with)
5 They make the pot bigger

138

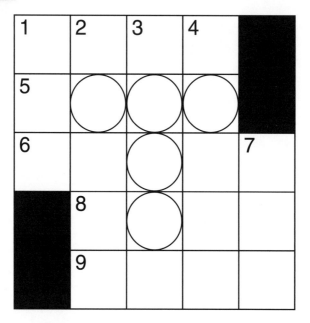

ACROSS
1 Poses a question
5 Org. with many Mideast members
6 Unbelievable people?
8 Hardware fastener . . . or a literal hint to the circled squares in this puzzle
9 Humpbacked ox of India

DOWN
1 Verizon purchase of 2015
2 Mark who won seven golds at the 1972 Summer Olympics
3 "The Family Circus" cartoonist Bil
4 Wash very hard
7 Letters between R and V

ACROSS

1 What Janet Yellen runs, with "the"

4 2007 title role for Ellen Page

5 "The ___ Project" (Hulu comedy)

6 Heavenly body?

7 Iron ___ (rust)

DOWN

1 Q: Why did the mushroom get invited to the party? A: Because he's a ___

2 Put a stop to

3 Creator of Holmes and Watson

4 "We just said the same thing!"

5 "Little Red Book" chairman

ACROSS

1 Creator of Watson, the memorable 2011 "Jeopardy!" winner
4 With 6- and 8-Across, entry that allows for later success
6 See 4-Across
8 See 4-Across
9 Praying surface

DOWN

1 "Don't mind ___ do!"
2 Ionic, covalent or metallic
3 The "M" of D.M.V.
5 Ten Commandments pronoun
7 Physics unit

ACROSS

1 "___: Days of Future Past" (2014 superhero movie)
5 Complete idiots
7 Its branch is a symbol for peace
8 Drug that treats panic attacks
9 Kick back and relax

DOWN

1 ___ One, video game console since 2013
2 Back tooth
3 Online-only publication
4 Exploding stars
6 R-rated message

142

ACROSS

1 Grumpy expression
6 First lady before Michelle
7 ___ of the world (elated)
8 Square dance venues
9 ___ flume (amusement park ride)

DOWN

1 Person who uses a sleeve for a napkin, say
2 Famous feature of Venice
3 Conclusion to a song
4 Incorrect
5 Swimmers' back-and-forths

ACROSS

1 Doorframe part
5 Virus spreader, at times
7 Sudden increase on a graph
8 Adjusts, as a guitar
9 Kid who keeps asking inane questions, e.g.

DOWN

1 "Surely you ___"
2 Energize
3 Largest state in New England
4 What the Wright Brothers originally made for a living
6 For fear that

144

ACROSS

1 Most common word in the English language ending in "U"
4 Lava lamp formations
6 Causing goosebumps
7 Kobe Bryant, e.g.
8 Most common word in the English language ending in "E"

DOWN

1 Radiohead lead singer Thom
2 New York theater award
3 _____ interface (programmer's concern)
4 Lap band?
5 Wife of Jacob, in the Bible

ACROSS

1 Brass = copper + ____

5 State whose panhandle touches Canada

7 Jay Z's competitor to Spotify

8 He cast the Killing Curse on Dumbledore

9 "Oh, and another thing . . ."

DOWN

1 Comic strip about a teenage boy

2 Menzel who won a Tony for "Wicked"

3 Winner of the most French Open singles titles

4 Cowboy's leggings

6 Butter substitute

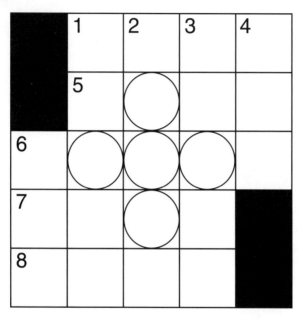

ACROSS

1 One of the Smurfs
5 Best hand in Texas Hold 'Em
6 Next year's sophs
7 Preeminent
8 "___ The Woods" (2014 Meryl Streep/Anna Kendrick movie)

DOWN

1 The smile or frown of an emoticon, for short
2 Come at ___
3 Sauce made with pine nuts
4 Volcanic fallout
6 Robert Mueller's former org.

ACROSS

1 "But ___ counting?"
5 Euphoric feelings
7 Like some record labels
8 Pet ___
9 Start of a football play

DOWN

1 Position for Frank Underwood on the first season of "House of Cards"
2 Cheryl of "Curb Your Enthusiasm"
3 Poet Nash
4 Hindu deity
6 Trickle

ACROSS

1 Media company with its own HBO show
5 Very friendly (with)
6 Spot of land in the sea
7 On the ___ (running amok)
8 Horse's gait

DOWN

1 Glare blocker in a car
2 Northern hemisphere?
3 Holder of pirate treasure
4 Suffix with kitchen or luncheon
5 Incline

	1	2	3	4
5				
6				
7				
8				

ACROSS

1 What Miss Wisconsin or Miss Wyoming wears
5 Like a scaredy-cat
6 Burglar's bane
7 Dunkin' Donuts order
8 "Ah! Say no more"

DOWN

1 Missile facilities
2 Flabbergast
3 Colorful Wonka candy
4 Song heard on Sunday morning
5 Dry riverbed

150

ACROSS

1 Command to a dog on a couch, maybe
4 Schick product
6 Something that wafts
7 ___ noir (red wine)
8 ___ kwon do

DOWN

1 O-O-O, chemically
2 Modern acronym for social anxiety
3 Seth Rogen's neighbors in the 2014 comedy "Neighbors"
4 Totally absorbed
5 Operatic solo

ANSWERS

1

P	S	A	■	H
H	E	L	L	O
I	N	L	A	W
S	T	A	N	D
H	■	H	E	Y

2

G	L	I	T	Z
R	I	B	■	Z
U	P	S	E	T
M	■	E	M	O
P	I	N	U	P

3

J	A	M	B	A
U	N	I	O	N
I	G	L	O	O
C	L	A	M	S
E	O	N	S	■

4

	J	O	A	N	
S	U	R	G	E	
I	L	I	E	D	
L	I	O	N	S	
K	A	N	T		

5

H	E	R	B	
T		A	I	M
T	I	Z	Z	Y
P	R	O		T
	A	R	C	H

6

	C	O	M	B
S	H	U		U
W	I	N	G	S
A		C	A	Y
B	E	E	S	

7

S	C	O	O	B
H	O	W	■	R
O	W	E	T	O
O	■	N	O	W
T	Y	S	O	N

8

■	H	U	G	■
S	E	V	E	N
P	L	U	T	O
A	P	L	U	S
■	S	A	P	■

9

■	G	P	A	■
F	R	A	C	K
A	O	R	T	A
T	O	K	E	N
■	M	A	D	■

I	S	L	E	S
K	M	A	R	T
N	I	T	R	O
O	T	T	E	R
W	E	E	D	Y

B	I	R	D	■
I	■	O	A	F
N	U	B	I	A
G	H	O	S	T
■	S	T	Y	E

E	S	S	A	Y
R	O	T	H	■
G	R	E	E	N
■	T	E	A	T
R	A	L	P	H

13

S	P	A		
H	A	W	K	S
I	T	M	A	Y
P	S	A	T	S
		N	Y	T

14

S	A	R	I	S
T	R	U	C	E
A	R	N	I	E
R	A	I	N	Y
Z	Y	N	G	A

15

	B	L	U	E
I	O	U		A
R	O	I	D	S
A		G	A	Y
Q	U	I	D	

16

R	A	M	S	
A	D	A	M	S
C	U	R	I	E
E	L	I	T	E
	T	E	E	N

17

T	H	I	N	
H	O	T	E	L
I	N	A	W	E
S	E	L	M	A
	D	Y	E	D

18

J	U	N	O	
E	P	O	C	H
S	P	I	C	Y
S	E	R	U	M
	D	E	R	N

19

P	I	Z	Z	A
R	■	L	E	G
O	Z	O	N	E
B	A	T	■	N
E	G	Y	P	T

20

F	■	X	A	S
A	B	A	B	A
T	E	N	E	T
S	T	A	T	S
O	S	X	■	■

21

D	I	V	V	Y
A	C	A	I	■
S	A	L	T	Y
■	L	U	A	U
S	L	E	E	P

22

F	R	I	S	K
R	E	N	T	A
A	C	T	O	N
N	O	W	A	Y
C	N	O	T	E

23

■	D	U	P	E
L	U	R	I	D
A	N	K	L	E
O	C	E	A	N
S	E	L	F	■

24

C	A	C	A	O
V	E	R	B	■
S	T	O	O	D
■	N	O	U	N
S	A	N	T	A

	S	N	A	G
	W	I	S	P
T	E	C	H	S
S	A	K	E	
K	R	I	S	

26

G	I	F	S	
E	L	E	C	
M	I	L	E	Y
	V	I	N	E
	E	X	E	S

27

	T	V	S	
J	U	I	C	E
A	P	R	E	S
M	A	G	N	A
	C	O	T	

28

C	U	P	I	D
O	I	L	■	A
H	E	A	R	T
E	■	N	Y	E
N	A	K	E	D

29

Y	O	U	■	S
A	S	N	A	P
C	H	I	N	A
H	A	T	E	R
T	■	E	W	E

30

■	A	C	T	S
■	M	A	I	L
Z	I	P	P	Y
A	G	E	S	■
G	O	R	Y	■

31

	B	A	T	H
C	A	C	H	E
U	S	H	E	R
B	I	O	M	E
S	L	O	E	

32

J	U	N	E	
U	P	E	N	N
A	T	A	R	I
N	O	T	O	K
	N	O	N	E

33

	A	U	N	T
A	N	N	I	E
L	Y	C	E	E
O		L	C	D
T	R	E	E	

34

	R	O	S	E
H	A	B	L	A
U	N	G	E	R
E	G	Y	P	T
S	Y	N	T	H

35

	N	A	B	
H	E	L	E	N
A	P	P	L	E
Y	A	H	O	O
	L	A	W	

36

	L	U	I	S
	A	N	N	E
Q	U	I	T	E
V	E	T	O	
C	R	E	W	

37

	A	N	T	I
	S	A	U	L
S	H	A	R	K
H	E	C	K	
U	S	P	S	

38

R	A	S	H	
A	L	O	E	
W	E	B	B	Y
	R	E	D	O
	T	R	O	N

39

	W	H	O	
W	H	E	N	
H	E	A	P	S
A	R	D	O	R
T	E	S	T	S

40

	L	B	S	
C	O	A	T	I
O	R	G	A	N
W	R	E	C	K
	E	L	K	

41

O	V	A	L	
S	I	R	I	
C	R	I	B	S
A	G	E	R	S
R	O	S	A	S

42

T	I	C	K	
A	C	U	R	A
N	O	T	A	X
K	N	I	F	E
	S	E	T	S

43

	C	O	L	A
P	U	N	I	C
A	T	O	N	E
L	E	F	T	S
S	Y	F	Y	

44

	E	L	S	A
B	R	E	W	S
A	N	N	E	S
B	I	D	E	N
Y	E	L	P	

45

	C	H	A	T
	H	A	I	R
F	I	L	M	Y
E	L	L	E	
D	I	E	D	

46

S	C	A	M	
K	O	B	E	
I	P	O	D	S
	T	R	I	P
	S	T	A	Y

47

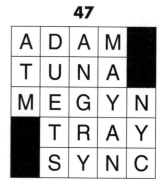

A	D	A	M	
T	U	N	A	
M	E	G	Y	N
	T	R	A	Y
	S	Y	N	C

48

	S	O	D	A
	C	O	E	D
C	U	Z	C	O
U	B	E	R	
E	A	S	Y	

49

	J	F	K	
R	I	L	E	D
A	H	O	R	A
M	A	U	R	Y
	D	R	Y	

50

B	R	B		
C	O	L	D	
C	L	E	A	R
	E	A	S	Y
		T	H	E

51

S	P	I	N	
E	L	M	O	
E	A	G	L	E
	C	A	T	S
	E	Y	E	S

52

	P	A	L	E
M	O	N	E	Y
A	L	G	A	E
T	A	L	K	S
T	R	E	S	

53

I	T	D		
D	R	E	S	S
K	A	F	K	A
	S	O	U	L
	H	E	A	T

54

	M	E	S	A
	A	X	I	S
S	M	I	T	H
A	B	L	E	
M	O	E	S	

55

I	F	F	Y	
P	O	R	E	S
A	G	O	N	Y
D	U	S	T	S
	P	H	A	T

56

	S	A	G	S
	K	N	U	T
P	I	D	A	Y
H	E	I	R	
I	D	E	D	

57

	F	O	O	D
	R	U	H	R
L	E	T	M	E
I	D	E	A	
P	O	R	N	

58

	I	M	O	K
	G	A	B	E
A	L	I	E	N
C	O	Z	Y	
T	O	E	S	

59

	F	I	D	O
P	R	M	E	N
A	I	S	L	E
S	E	A	T	S
O	D	D	S	

60

C	H	I	L	E
L	O	V	E	R
I	R	A	T	E
M	S	N	B	C
B	E	S	E	T

61

A	D	H	D	█
B	O	E	R	█
S	P	A	D	E
█	E	R	R	S
█	S	T	E	P

62

█	T	E	M	P
█	H	A	A	S
J	E	R	R	Y
E	E	L	S	█
B	U	S	H	█

63

M	U	S	T	S
I	N	P	U	T
S	A	U	N	A
E	G	R	E	T
R	I	N	S	E

64

	S	N	A	P
	T	O	G	A
N	E	V	E	R
E	V	E	N	
W	E	L	T	

65

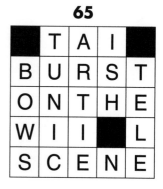

	T	A	I	
B	U	R	S	T
O	N	T	H	E
W	I	I		L
S	C	E	N	E

66

	B	E	N	Z	
A	Q	U	A	
S	U	R	G	E
	A	S	A	P
	L	E	T	S

67

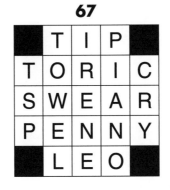

	T	I	P	
T	O	R	I	C
S	W	E	A	R
P	E	N	N	Y
	L	E	O	

68

	S	P	A	S
	P	I	N	K
D	I	N	G	Y
A	N	T	E	
Y	E	A	R	

69

	P	U	C	K
D	U	B	A	I
O	P	E	D	S
F	A	R	E	S
F	E	S	T	

70

	P	J	S	
F	A	U	N	A
O	N	I	O	N
B	A	C	O	N
	M	E	T	

71

	A	S	I	F
	P	I	N	E
	K	O	O	K	Y
G	L	U	E	
B	O	X	Y	

72

S	M	U	T	
M	I	L	A	N
U	N	T	I	E
G	I	R	L	S
	S	A	S	S

73

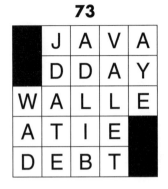

	J	A	V	A
	D	D	A	Y
W	A	L	L	E
A	T	I	E	
D	E	B	T	

74

	M	A	R	K
B	A	T	H	E
R	I	S	E	N
I	N	I	T	S
T	E	X	T	

75

P	A	Y	T	V
S	A	M	O	A
I	N	C	A	N
	D	A	D	
	E	S	S	

76

F	I	L	A	
U	N	U	M	
N	E	X	U	S
	P	O	S	H
	T	R	E	Y

77

	M	A	H	I
W	A	L	E	S
W	H	I	R	L
J	E	T	T	A
D	R	O	Z	

78

A	D	A	P	T
S	E	D	E	R
P	L	A	T	E
C	A	G	E	S
A	Y	E	R	S

79

W	I	F	I	
E	D	U	C	E
S	I	D	E	A
T	O	G	A	S
	T	E	X	T

80

	A	P	P	S
	C	O	O	K
G	O	T	B	Y
O	R	T	O	
O	N	Y	X	

81

A	G	T		
S	L	I	D	E
H	O	M	E	R
	V	E	R	A
G	E	R	M	S

82

	G	N	U	
	D	R	U	G
T	R	U	T	H
H	U	M	S	
U	M	P		

83

	N	E	E	D
V	O	L	V	O
A	T	T	I	C
S	M	O	C	K
T	E	N	T	S

84

	C	T	S	
S	A	R	A	H
A	R	U	B	A
M	O	L	L	Y
	B	Y	E	

85

T	V	P	G	
L	I	O	N	
C	O	L	O	N
	L	A	M	B
	A	R	E	A

86

E	C	I	G	
A	R	B	O	R
R	A	I	M	I
S	I	Z	E	S
	G	A	Z	E

87

		G	U	N
M	I	A	M	I
A	R	Y	A	N
T	I	L	D	E
S	S	E		

88

	B	E	C	K
W	A	X	O	N
E	M	C	E	E
A	B	O	D	E
R	I	P	S	

89

B	Y	L	A	W
L	E	E		H
A	T	A	R	I
C		R	A	T
K	A	N	Y	E

90

	G	E	N	
G	E	N	O	A
A	N	J	O	U
B	R	O	N	X
	E	Y	E	

	P	A	S	T
M	O	T	T	O
A	B	O	U	T
R	O	N	D	O
E	X	E	S	

	S	A	M	
C	E	D	A	R
O	N	E	P	M
L	O	L	L	S
T	R	E	E	

J	A	Z	Z	
A	W	A	I	T
B	E	I	G	E
S	E	R	G	E
	K	E	Y	S

94

	H	O	W	L
M	A	R	I	O
A	N	G	E	R
R	O	A	L	D
K	I	N	D	

95

H	O	R	S	E
B	L	U	E	
O	I	L	E	D
	V	E	R	Y
V	E	R	S	E

96

	F	L	A	N
P	I	E		E
R	E	M	I	X
O		O	C	T
D	I	N	E	

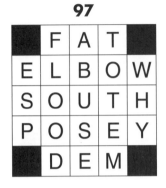

	F	A	T	
E	L	B	O	W
S	O	U	T	H
P	O	S	E	Y
	D	E	M	

U	T	A	H	
R	E	B	E	L
I	R	O	N	Y
S	P	U	R	N
	S	T	Y	X

	W	H	I	M
	H	A	T	E
M	Y	M	A	N
A	M	A	L	
D	E	N	Y	

100

J	I	M	I	
I	R	A	N	
B	A	N	D	O
	Q	U	I	D
	I	P	A	D

101

A	D	M	I	T
T	R	U	N	K
L	A	S	S	O
	F	E	U	D
S	T	E	M	

102

		T	A	G
	C	O	R	N
C	H	A	M	P
H	E	S	S	
E	X	T		

103

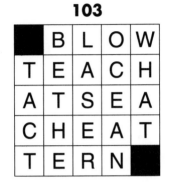

	B	L	O	W
T	E	A	C	H
A	T	S	E	A
C	H	E	A	T
T	E	R	N	

104

M	A	S	S	
O	V	U	M	
N	E	P	A	L
	R	E	Z	A
	T	R	E	X

105

	O	N	U	S
Q	U	A	N	T
U	T	U	B	E
A	R	R	O	W
D	E	U	X	

106

	D	I	A	L
L	I	N	G	O
A	N	D	O	R
M	A	I	N	E
P	R	E	Y	

107

	A	H	H	
F	L	O	Y	D
A	I	R	E	R
M	A	N	N	Y
	S	E	A	

108

	T	S	K	
A	H	O	Y	S
M	R	F	O	X
C	O	A	T	S
	B	R	O	W

112

	D	I	S	C
F	E	T	C	H
A	L	G	A	E
U	T	U	R	N
N	A	Y	S	

113

	J	L	O	
G	O	O	F	Y
P	L	U	T	O
A	L	I	E	N
	Y	E	N	

114

S	P	A	M	
T	I	P	U	P
E	X	T	R	A
P	A	N	S	Y
	R	O	E	S

115

116

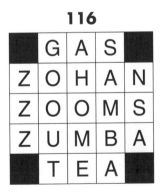

117

118

	B	U	S	
R	E	N	T	S
M	A	J	O	R
S	C	A	R	S
	H	M	M	

119

P	C	B		
A	O	R	T	A
P	R	O	W	L
A	N	N	I	E
		X	X	X

120

	A	P	P	S
	C	H	A	I
I	H	O	P	E
N	O	T	A	
K	O	O	L	

121

	C	D	C	
T	R	E	A	D
B	A	L	M	Y
S	W	I	P	E
P	L	A	Y	S

122

A	B	C		
R	A	Z	Z	
T	H	E	U	N
	A	C	L	U
	H	U	T	

123

	Z	A	P	S
K	O	R	E	A
O	R	I	N	G
C	R	A	N	E
H	O	L	Y	

124

	G	D	S	
P	H	O	T	O
R	A	Z	O	R
O	N	E	I	L
F	A	N	C	Y

125

S	E	W	O	N
P	I	A	N	O
A	G	N	E	W
M	E	D	I	A
S	R	S	L	Y

126

	M	G	M	
C	A	R	O	M
A	L	O	N	E
B	L	U	T	H
	S	P	Y	

127

K	O	A	L	A
A		X	E	R
P	O	L	A	R
U	N	E		A
T	E	D	D	Y

128

	S	H	O	P
	T	O	U	R
P	O	U	T	Y
A	R	S	E	
W	E	E	D	

129

	A	L	M	S
	G	O	U	P
T	I	M	M	Y
B	L	A	M	
D	E	N	Y	

130

A	M	T	O	O
R	E	A	L	M
M	A	R	I	E
■	L	O	N	G
■	■	T	E	A

131

■	■	O	H	H
D	E	F	O	E
A	D	A	M	S
L	U	G	E	S
■	■	E	R	E

132

S	K	E	W	S
P	A	L	E	O
A	S	L	A	N
S	H	I	V	A
M	I	S	E	R

136

	B	R	E	R
	L	E	V	I
J	A	C	O	B
I	M	O	K	
G	E	N	E	

137

	S	P	O	T
B	O	R	N	E
E	L	I	T	E
T	V	M	O	M
S	E	P	P	

138

A	S	K	S	
O	P	E	C	
L	I	A	R	S
	T	N	U	T
	Z	E	B	U

139

		F	E	D
	J	U	N	O
M	I	N	D	Y
A	N	G	E	L
O	X	I	D	E

140

I	B	M		
F	O	O	T	
I	N	T	H	E
	D	O	O	R
		R	U	G

141

X	M	E	N	
B	O	Z	O	S
O	L	I	V	E
X	A	N	A	X
	R	E	S	T

142

S	C	O	W	L
L	A	U	R	A
O	N	T	O	P
B	A	R	N	S
	L	O	G	

143

J	A	M	B	
E	M	A	I	L
S	P	I	K	E
T	U	N	E	S
	P	E	S	T

144

		Y	O	U
B	L	O	B	S
E	E	R	I	E
L	A	K	E	R
T	H	E		

Z	I	N	C	
I	D	A	H	O
T	I	D	A	L
S	N	A	P	E
	A	L	S	O

146

	P	A	P	A
	A	C	E	S
F	R	O	S	H
B	E	S	T	
I	N	T	O	

147

W	H	O	S	
H	I	G	H	S
I	N	D	I	E
P	E	E	V	E
	S	N	A	P

148

	V	I	C	E
T	I	G	H	T
I	S	L	E	T
L	O	O	S	E
T	R	O	T	

149

	S	A	S	H
W	I	M	P	Y
A	L	A	R	M
D	O	Z	E	N
I	S	E	E	

150

		O	F	F
R	A	Z	O	R
A	R	O	M	A
P	I	N	O	T
T	A	E		

Looking for more Hard Crosswords?

The New York Times

The #1 Name in Crosswords

Looking for more Large-Print Crosswords?

The New York Times

The #1 Name in Crosswords

Looking for more Sunday Crosswords?

The New York Times

The #1 Name in Crosswords